Society for Promoting Manual Training

Berlin Course of Easy Wood-Work

Society for Promoting Manual Training

Berlin Course of Easy Wood-Work

ISBN/EAN: 9783337389147

Printed in Europe, USA, Canada, Australia, Japan

Cover: Foto ©Paul-Georg Meister /pixelio.de

More available books at **www.hansebooks.com**

BERLIN COURSE

OF

EASY WOOD-WORK

AN INTRODUCTION TO
PRACTICAL WORK FOR YOUNGER BOYS
IN SCHOOL AND HOME

With an Appendix

Containing the Course of the Berlin School-Workshop in
Paper, Cardboard, and Stick Work

WITH 260 SKETCHES ON 11 PLATES

ISSUED BY THE SOCIETY FOR PROMOTING MANUAL TRAINING
BERLIN SECTION

Translated by W. G. FIELD, M.A.

LONDON
O. NEWMANN & CO., 84 Newman Street, W.
1895

Preface

In the formation of courses, the German advocates of Manual Training are guided by two principles: on the one hand, they seek to adapt the work to be done to the physical strength, intellectual development, and interests of the child; on the other, they endeavour so to arrange it that there is a clear progression from the easy to the difficult, and from the simple to the composite.

The little book before me fills a gap in the courses based on this system which are already in existence. Practical teachers have long felt the presence of such a gap; it was necessary to find for boys of from eight to ten years of age some form of employment exactly suited to the stage at which they are, some means of quickening and developing the desire of activity, and the formative impulse. The Introduction which follows elucidates this in the light of facts and of history.

Referring, then, to that Introduction, in the first place, as President of the chief Berlin Association for Promoting the Manual Training of Boys, I testify that Easy Wood-Work has fully approved its value in the Berlin school-workshops, and attracts proportionally the greatest number of pupils. It awakens the desire to work and the delight in work; it trains eye, hand, and form-sense of the boy in a way adapted to his youthful capacity, and it proves an excellent bridge to the more serious and difficult work done at the bench.

Anyone who reads the following explanatory remarks on the method of conducting the instruction, and observes the great multiplicity of objects and forms represented in the plates, will become conscious that this course has been drawn up with much thought and care, and has grown under the test of actual experience. Thus in our Berlin Association we are grateful to those who have performed with so much industry and devotion the meritorious task of preparing it. Our feelings are shared by many teachers who at the Danzig Congress this year examined the work done in accordance with this course.

I may therefore wish this little book a very wide circulation. It will assuredly be welcome everywhere where the want of suitable employment, educational in its character, for boys of the age indicated is felt, particularly then in workshops for the young, working homes, orphanages, reformatories, and other educational institutions. Nor will it be less available for the home circle. I warmly commend it for use in all such quarters.

VON SCHENCKENDORFF,
Member of the Abgeordneten-Haus, President of the Berlin Association, and of the German Association for Promoting Manual Training.

GÖRLITZ, *October* 1894.

Contents

	PAGE
PREFACE	3
INTRODUCTION	7
THE METHOD OF CONDUCTING THE WORK	13
COURSES :—	
A. WORK WITH "NATURAL" WOOD	23
B. WORK WITH SPLIT-WOOD AND THIN BOARDS	32
APPENDIX :—	
COURSE IN PAPER, CARDBOARD, AND STICK WORK	42

Introduction

THE present movement in favour of enlisting work with the body in the service of education received, as is well known, its first impetus from Denmark and Sweden. Now, as the northern Slöjd is, in the main, confined to wood-work at the bench, which naturally can only be pursued with advantage by boys more than eleven years old, in the first German workshops for the young, that was the age which was kept in view. The practical courses in "pulp" work, wood-carving, bench work, and metal work, were throughout calculated only for older boys. But the more the conviction grew that, to satisfy the child's innate impulse to activity, and to secure the full harmonious development of its powers, practical work must be added as a necessary complement to the educational disciplines hitherto employed, the plainer it became to the advocates of Manual Training that no age should be excluded from the benefits of the instruction. This opinion derived confirmation from the fact that in *Kindergärten* the principle of work was beneficially applied in the case of children of the preparatory school age. Thus the wish to fill the gap —to form a bridge, as it were—between the work of the Kindergarten and the school-workshop grew stronger. The matter engaged the attention of the German Association for the Promotion of Manual Training. At its fifth general meeting at Eisenach in 1891, Herr Hertel and

Herr Kalb delivered addresses which formed the basis of an exhaustive discussion of the subject. The result of that discussion was a recommendation to all German school-workshops to make practical experiments in order to throw light on the form courses should take to be most suitable for younger children.

Suggestions for such experiments lay ready to hand in many books. Thus the labours of Barth and Niederley (*Des deutschen Knaben Handwerksbuch*), Elm (*Spiel und Arbeit*) Seidel and Schmidt (*Arbeitsschule*), Fellner (*Formenarbeiten*) and Georgens (*Das geometrische Ausschneiden*) afforded valuable hints; moreover, several institutions, such as the Dresden School-Workshops, many schools for children of defective powers, and a number of Children's Homes, had endeavoured to realise in practice the suggestions made.

Nor had similar efforts been wanting in the northern countries; the same desire for more elementary work had been operative there for some years. But whilst in Germany the material adopted for the transition stage had been chiefly paper and cardboard, or, in a limited measure, straw, cane, and shavings, in the north they still clung to wood as the most appropriate substance with which even the younger boys could work. Eva Rodhe[1] of Gothenburg, and Vera Hjelt[2] of Helsingfors, have drawn up and published a complete course of wood-work for children of from five to ten years of age. In like manner, Aksel Mikkelsen makes children who have passed their fifth year begin exercises in wood. Nor can it be denied that it is extremely desirable and advantageous to offer even our younger boys wood to work with in a suitable way; even though it is, in our judgment, necessary that they should first have tried their strength on some material, such as paper or cardboard, which offers less resistance, and so have prepared themselves in a sense

---

[1] Eva Rodhe, *Modellserien für Holzslöjd*.
[2] Vera Hjelt, *Slöjdläraren för de små*.

for work of greater difficulty. Now, as the three northern advocates of Easy Wood-Work introduce too many tools— Mikkelsen, indeed, employs bench-work tools which can be used with profit only by boys of thirteen or fourteen— and as they consequently set the child to tasks which are too advanced for its years, we cannot in Germany follow their lead, whilst we recognise, nevertheless, the value of wood as a material even for very young boys. Thus we are driven to devising for ourselves such forms of wood-work *as require but few tools, and as are not beyond the powers and ideas of boys from eight to eleven years of age*.

The merit of taking the first step in this direction belongs to Herr Kalb of Gera. In the *Knabenhort* which he controls, he caused small objects to be made from pine twigs and split firewood. Specimens of the work so produced were exhibited by him to the meeting at Eisenach, of which mention has already been made. Soon afterwards they were examined and discussed by the Berlin Association of Schoolmasters for Encouraging Manual Training. The work was much approved, and, at the suggestion of the Association, the Easy Exercises in Wood were adopted in the winter plan of the Berlin workshops (1891-92) as a "Second Preparatory Stage" for boys from eight to eleven years old. The many applications from pupils to be allowed to take the course was the best proof possible that it supplied a general want.

At the outset these elementary courses were based on Herr Kalb's designs. Alterations and additions were gradually introduced by the various teachers of the subject. The work done in the winter half-year was well received by the public, to whom every Easter an exhibition of the products of our workshops is opened. At the eleventh German Congress for Educational Handicraft, held at Frankfurt am Main in 1892, the examples of our "Easy Wood-Work" offered for inspection gained the approval of experts. In the two years which have elapsed since then, our system has been more fully developed. We have not only increased the number of our models, and so given greater variety to the work, but we have also endeavoured to arrange them in a certain sequence according to the method of construction. In ordering them, we have been governed by the pedagogic principles—" From the easy to the difficult," and " From the simple to the composite." The gradation we have thus obtained, extending now to more than two hundred models, was again highly appreciated at the Danzig Congress in the present year, where, as at Frankfurt, our specimens were exhibited.

Even before that exhibition many Manual teachers had expressed a wish that the Berlin " Easy Wood-Work " should be made accessible to other institutions. And as at Danzig that wish was found to be general, the Association felt bound to meet it. We therefore appointed a commission to publish, in text and plates, the course as arranged at Berlin. The text gives, in a few brief words, the explanations necessary for the construction of the object. The dimensions suggested need not in every case be exactly observed ; nevertheless it will be advisable, in general, to maintain the proportions indicated by those dimensions, because they correspond in some degree to reality. We give the sketches, which, in default of a model, supply the idea of the object, on separate plates. They can thus be mounted and hung up in the workshop or school-room.

It will readily be understood that the course here prescribed need not under all circumstances be followed undeviatingly. Rather will the thoughtful teacher here and there, as occasion and locality require, omit or change a task, or substitute some other object. The little book is, above all, intended to furnish the teacher with an opportunity of becoming acquainted with this form of elementary work, in order that he may test it with boys of the age set down. The employment is quite in keeping with the nature of children, who, from their earliest years, love to hammer and to cut. And experience has shown that boys apply themselves to the work with zest and delight. We trust, then, that the book will not only find admission into school-workshops, Boys' Homes, and educational institutions generally, but that it will be a welcome counsellor to boys who have already gained some knowledge of the means of self-employment.

We would here anticipate the objection which now and then is raised, that no educational value attaches to this simple work. Our conviction, ratified by experience, is that these elementary courses are well calculated to exert that beneficial influence which is claimed for all well-directed Manual Work. Our "Easy Wood-Work" teaches the child chiefly to make toys, and to reproduce on a small scale what he sees about him in life. Every student of child-nature, and every observer of children's games, will bear witness that what we offer is just what the child wants, that it suits its natural impulses. But this wood-work does not merely gratify, it also requires accurate observation of the things of everyday life: it stimulates the imagination in the right degree; it requires careful measurement, correctness in estimating, a skilful handling of knife and hammer. It makes the young hand dexterous, and awakens a sense for symmetrical and beautiful shapes. The simple tasks bring the goal of accomplishment near, and the possibility of speedily attaining it delights the little workman, strengthens his will, and draws his mind from the visionary to the possible.

In an Appendix we present, for the sake of completeness, a course in paper, cardboard, and stick work, forming the "First Preparatory Stage" in the Berlin school-workshops. The work so suggested is intended to follow immediately the practical "occupations" of the Kindergarten, and to lead up to the "Easy Wood-Work" which is our "Second Preparatory Stage."

We give, then, our little book to publicity, with the hope

that it will contribute its share to the internal development of Manual Training, a discipline which daily gains wider recognition, and attracts new adherents to its support.

The Commission of the Association,
LIPS, FRENKEL, GRANBERG, GROPPLER, ROSENBERG.

BERLIN, *September* 1894.

Of the Manner of Carrying on the Work

To carry on Easy Wood-Work requires neither costly fittings, nor numerous and expensive tools. Any ordinary table can be converted into a work-table, by laying on it a board planed smooth. It is advisable to secure the board to the table by screw-clamps (wood screws). If there is a special room for a considerable number of boys available, we lay planks, 60 to 70 cm. wide, across wooden trestles. A sketch of one of these trestles, which resemble the vaulting-blocks used in gymnasiums, is given in Plate 7, Fig. 16. The height of the trestles must vary according to the size of the boys. As the boys stand whilst working, the satisfactory height for those of from eight to ten years of age will, in general, be 75—85 cm. If the work-table is too high, the boy cannot bring his full strength to bear as he cuts. To stand firmly, the trestles must have four legs. Eight of these trestles, together with four planks, each 3 m. long, would cost about £3 or £3, 10s. If we wish to adapt the school-room during out-of-school hours to a workshop, we may lay the planks across the desks, or still better, we may place low wooden stands on the forms, and rest the planks on these. Such arrangements are found in at least three of the Berlin school-workshops.

The tools needed are — knife, hammer, bradawl, ruler, pincers, fretsaw, file, compasses, and sawing-board. Each pupil must have the first four of these; of the others a certain number will suffice for the whole class or division.

Various forms of knife have been recommended. Any ordinary pocket-knife will serve the purpose; but best of all are the two patterns of Slöjd knife. In Fig. 1 we show a knife such as basket-makers use; it is very suitable for our work, and costs in Germany about 9d.

If the work is to be successful, the knives must constantly be kept sharp. They are best and most easily sharpened on a grindstone. In the absence thereof we may use a quadrangular piece of sandstone—what is called in Germany a Rutscher. The price of a Rutscher is 2s. 6d.

When the knives have been ground, they must be set on an oilstone (price 1s.). Let the children see how this operation is performed.

As in Easy Wood-Work only small nails and brads are employed, a little hammer costing 10d. will suffice.

To make holes, choose a bradawl at a price of 3d. The handle should not be too small. The use of the bradawl is to bore holes for nails, which thus receive their true direction, while the splitting of the wood is avoided.

Rulers must be of firm wood, and marked with centimetre divisions. A length of 25 to 30 cm. will be enough. (Price, per dozen, 6s.)

To pull out bent nails or those which have gone askew, we need pincers (price 1s.), or flat-jawed pliers (price 8d.). If the pincers have sharp edges, we can use them to nip off projecting points of nails. But we usually have special *nippers* for the purpose. We may also beat over projecting points with the hammer; when this is done, a strip of hoop-iron, 8 cm. long, or indeed any piece of iron, placed under the head of the nail, will render good service.

The dearest tool is the fretsaw, and it would be a mistake to stint expenditure when buying it. The cheap kinds become unfit for use in a very short time. For

Of the Manner of Carrying on the Work

3s. we can get a good, durable fretsaw frame (Fig. 2). The complete tool consists of the frame (*a*), the two screw-clamps (*bb*), the handle (*c*), and the blade (*d*). The frame may be of wood, steel, or iron. Wooden frames are for the most part to be preferred to iron. The former are, it is true, dearer than the latter, but they last longer. For our purpose, a size measured from one screw-clamp to the other, of 20—25 cm., will be long enough.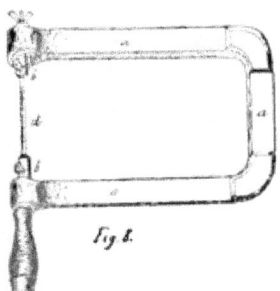

Very serviceable are the iron frames which have the two arms close together, and are so contrived that the saw-blade may project above the upper clamp. Thus, if a piece of the blade becomes broken off, the whole need not be thrown away.

Each clamp has two cheeks, ribbed on the inside. The blade of the saw is gripped between the two cheeks by means of a screw. As the clamps generally end in a screw, the distance between them can be varied. The lower clamp is connected with the wooden handle. The blade is a strip of steel, the thickness of which varies according to circumstances. The teeth are all inclined in the same direction. Nos. 2 and 3 are the fretsaw blades which are most suitable for Easy Wood-Work.

To fix the blade in position, press the upper arm of the frame against the edge of the table, so that the clamps move toward each other. Then screw the blade tightly in at top and bottom, in such a way that the teeth point outwards and downwards towards the handle. To screw the clamps tightly up, use the pliers.

For the proper use of the fretsaw for all purposes we also need a cutting-board, on which the wood to be sawed lies. The usual form of cutting board, as shown in Fig. 3, consists of a board 20—24 cm. long, and 12—15 cm. wide (beech or alder is the best wood), with a triangular piece cut out. This board is joined by a dovetail to a firm handscrew, by means of which it can be fixed on to any ordinary table. The price of a cutting-board with strong handscrew is 1s.

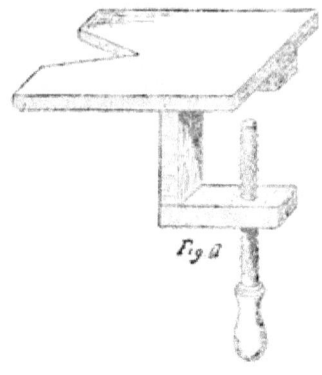

As in case of careless usage by the boy the arm in which the screw works is likely to split, we have caused cutting-boards to be constructed without handscrews (Fig. 4). In these the board (a) rests on a fairly stout stand (b), 20 cm. long, which at its upper end has a dovetail incision to receive the cross-strip (c). The board is joined both to the stand and to the cross-strip by screws. The stand has two wooden bars mortised into it (two tenons with open mortises). The upper of these has two incisions made to receive the wooden wedges (cc). The bars lie, one above, the other below, the top of the work-table, and the whole cutting-board is held in position by means of the wedges. To prevent the wedges from being lost, they may be attached to the stand by chains, as shown in the sketch.

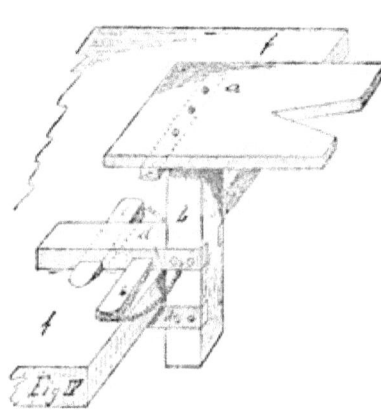

If the planks on which the boys work lie free on wooden trestles, a cutting-board may be used of the pattern shown in Fig. 5. At such a cutting-board two boys can work at the same time. A piece of board, 15-20 cm. wide, and 40 cm. longer than the breadth of the work-table,

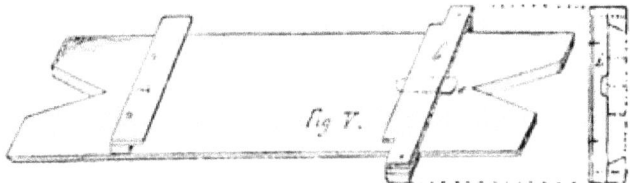

fig. V.

has a triangular incision made at either end, and on its longer sides is pared away (bevelled); 20 cm. from the end of the board we screw on a strip of wood with a projecting ledge (*a*). Another strip (*b*), the construction of which will be plain from the drawing, fits over the other end of the board, but so that it can be moved to and fro. The latter strip is set as the width of the work-table requires, then secured in its position by a wedge (*c*).

During the sawing the left hand holds the wood that is being cut firmly on to the cutting-board. The blade of the saw must be worked gently up and down in the cut (cerf) in a vertical direction. Care must be taken that the saw is not pressed hard and not turned sidewards.

The troublesome dust produced by fretsaw work has caused many protests to be raised against the use of this tool in Manual Work for boys. As with us the fretsaw is only an auxiliary, as it is only used to cut the outlines of the boards used in various pieces of work, there can be no question of such an amount of dust as to be injurious to health. Perforated work, fretsaw work proper, is excluded from our course. If a saw called a "marquetry" saw, having a much thicker blade than the common fretsaw, is employed, the quantity of the dust is considerably diminished.

To set out the outlines of the little boards, the pupil sometimes needs a pair of compasses, best with a lead pencil fitted in. The boys must bring their own compasses, as also lead pencils. Or we may buy, as part of the fitting out of the workshop, a pair of true, carefully-made iron compasses with steel points.

It must be a strictly observed rule that the pupils *draw for themselves*—they must not trace from patterns—whatever has to be drawn in the course of the work. Where curves and undulating lines occur which cannot be described with the compasses, they must be drawn with the unassisted hand. We naturally do not make very great demands on a child's skill in this direction.

The file is an instrument made of hardened steel, its surface being broken by a number of small cuts. The steel is fitted into a handle. The tool is used to remove inequalities on cut surfaces. We employ for our work either the half-round file (⌒), or the flat wood-file with rectangular cross-section (▭). In filing, the board is held fast on the table with the left hand, in such a way that the edge to be smoothed is parallel to the edge of the table, and projects somewhat beyond it. The last polish is given to a cut surface with sand or glass paper. The paper is sold under various numbers, No. 0 being the finest. We use Nos. 1, 2, and 3. The best plan is to wrap the sandpaper about a smoothly planed board, hold the board firmly on the work-table, and pass the edge to be finished to and fro over it. The paper may also be simply laid on the level table and the same process pursued.

To test the accuracy of a right angle on a sawed board, a try square should be employed. Such a square consists of two wooden arms (or one wooden and one steel arm) set immovably at a true right angle.

The Easy Wood-Work of the Berlin school-workshops falls into two sections:—

(1) Work done with "natural" wood (in the winter half-year).

(2) Work done with split-wood and thin boards (in the summer half-year).

The requisite material can easily be procured anywhere.

By "natural" wood, we mean twigs just as they are taken from trees and shrubs. The willow, the alder, the hazel, the pine, as also our fruit-trees, all yield suitable material. It will be well at the commencement to work with the softest possible wood, and not to pass to the harder kinds until later, when the hand of the pupil has gained more skill. Twigs with a wide medullary sheath are not suitable for Easy Wood-Work, as they easily split, and nails do not get a firm grip in them. If the nails are to be knocked into the sheath, little wedges about the thickness of a match must first be driven into the pith: otherwise, the nails will not hold.

The twigs cut from trees and shrubs in the late autumn should be bought up, left for some time to dry, and then used. If wood is green when worked, it afterwards dries and shrinks, and the objects made with it are ruined. That is why work from "natural" wood is done in winter, when the twigs have had time to dry.

Cane, the thin twigs of the *calamus rotang*, is also well suited for our purpose, since, in consequence of its pliancy, it allows a freer treatment of form. Its comparatively high price is, however, a restriction upon its extensive employment.

For work with split-wood, pieces of dry red or white deal, free from knots, such wood as is used by the cooper, will be found best. The boys receive pieces 10, 15, or 30 cm. long, and as thick as ordinary firewood chips, to be split by them into smaller sticks. To smooth the chips, use file and sandpaper. Or they may be scraped with a piece of glass; but then great care is requisite, for the glass may break and cut the hand.

Small wire nails or brads serve to join the sticks together. The two first sizes are generally needed, 13 mm. and 20 mm.; only in rare cases larger sizes, 25–30 mm. The nails are bought by the packet at a trifling cost. The rule should be: If you drive a nail into the pith, take a long one, and first wedge the pith as we have explained. If two sticks are to be nailed to each other across and through the pith, choose a shorter nail and hammer the point over, the head resting on a strip of iron. Often you must drive two nails in for the sake of greater firmness.

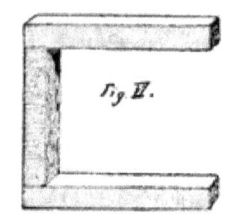

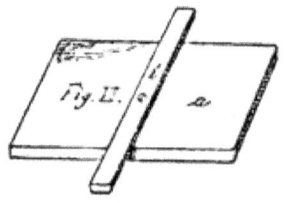

With some objects—for example, with those shown in Figs. 34, 58, and 59—it is necessary to hang the work on a frame, so that whilst knocking a nail into one side we may avoid pressing the other together. For this purpose we avail ourselves of the outer part of a wooden handscrew (Fig. 6). Lacking that, we may simply lay a long four-edged stick (b) over the work-table (a) so that it projects some 20 cm. at either side. The stick is fastened in the middle to the table by a nail (Fig. 8).

To allow ourselves to introduce greater variety into our work, whether it be done with "natural" or with split wood, we bring into service small boards cut with the fretsaw. The wood most suitable for these is alder, lime, or maple. But birch, walnut, and the wood of many fruit trees may also be used, as also cigar boxes, the wood of the Virginian cedar. Most frequently we choose alder, 3–5 mm. thick, and planed on both sides. A list of woods with prices is contained in Herr Kalb's book, to which reference has before been made.

Special sticks may be bought for certain kinds of work, at a cost of 6d. a hundred.

An improved appearance may be given to the work by bronzing, colouring, or applying a *Waldmosaik* (see A. Fig. 55), or by using brass-headed nails and ribbons. Some objects may be interwoven with strips of coloured paper, or bast; others, such as cradles, beds, tents, etc., may be covered with cotton stuff.

Gold bronze is obtained either in glass tubes or in small packets. In the former case, water is used as a solvent; in the latter, a special "bronze tincture." When dissolved, the bronze is spread on the work with a small soft camel's hair brush. Water "gilding" has to be laid on in a double coat, and does not last so well as bronzing with the tincture.

The only wood that is coloured is split-wood, or "natural" wood from which the bark has been stripped. For colouring we use brunoline, aniline, or wood stains. These should be bought in fluid form as they are required.

Decoration by means of *Waldmosaik*, if it is to be successful, calls for both practice and taste. If such ornamentation is to produce a good effect, it must be applied sparingly. Suitable for the purpose are: dried grasses, lichens, mosses, birch bark, acorns, beechnuts, the scales of fir cones, or small cones, which again may also be bronzed and wound about with ribbons and bows.

As many teachers desire to know the cost of an outfit for a class or division of pupils, we append an estimate for twenty-four pupils engaged in Easy Wood-Work.

	£	s.	d.
Eight (or four) wooden trestles, with four boards to lay over them . from	3	10	0
One large saw	0	3	0
Half-dozen cutting-boards, @ 1s. .	0	6	0
Half-dozen fretsaw frames, @ 3s. .	0	18	0
Two dozen knives, @ 10s. 6d. per doz.	1	1	0
Two dozen hammers, @ 10s. per doz .	1	0	0
One dozen bradawls, @ 3s. per doz. .	0	3	0
Two dozen rulers, @ 6s. per doz. .	0	12	0
One pair pincers	0	1	0
Two pairs flat-jawed pliers, @ 8d. each	0	1	4

	£	s.	d.
One " Rutscher "	0	2	6
One oilstone	0	1	0
One gross fretsaws (blades), @ 10d. per doz.	0	10	0
Sandpaper	0	2	0
Wire nails or brads (small sizes)	0	0	8

Course

(*Note.*—The numbers express the dimensions in centimetres.
L. = length ; B = breadth ; H = height.)

A. Work with Wood in its Natural State.

(Plates I–VI.)

1st Group.—The Cutting of Simple Sticks.

PRELIMINARY EXERCISES: (*a*) The pupils cut several sticks, 3 cm. long. The twig just as brought from the garden is laid on the table; the left hand, which holds the twig, must not touch the table. The knife is pressed down vertically with the right hand, the twig rolled forward with the left hand. If the stick is very thick, we may make in the same way an incision all round it, then snap off with the fingers. The cut surfaces must be smoothed. (Practice in vertical cutting of a stick.)

(*b*) Several sticks 10 cm. long are cut, and pointed like pencils. The left hand grasps the "pencil," the right makes the cuts in a direction *away from* the body.

(*c*) The pencil lies in the left hand, its head on the thumb. The knife in the right hand, directed *towards* the body, shapes the point. (Practice in pointing.)

Fig. 1. *Flower-stick.* — H. 25. The stick is measured with the rule and cut off to the length desired; a long point is made at the bottom; the top is rounded off; below the top a notch is cut all round. (Head and neck.) In use the long point is thrust into the earth, the flowers are tied to the stick. Thus the thicker part of the stick should be the part towards the bottom, where greater strength is required.

Fig. 2. Pennon.—H. 25. The stick receives "head and neck," as in Fig. 1; it is split for about 7 cm. of its length, and a piece of coloured paper cut into a swallow's tail is inserted in the slit; nail together with two nails; hammer down the points of the nails. The paper may also be glued to the stick. Use to decorate the Christmas tree.

Fig. 3. Banner.— H. 25; cross-piece L. 7. Make "head and neck"; glue a paper flag to the cross-piece; hang cross-piece to neck with thin twine.

Fig. 4. Dart.—L. 30. The point may be made with a headless nail or a bit of wire pointed. Be careful where you throw your dart! At the top two slits are made at right angles to each other to a depth of 5 cm., and the folded paper inserted therein. To make the paper part, take a piece of paper 12 cm. square; fold it over in the diagonals and middle lines to right and left; now lay either the adjacent or the opposite corners on one another.

2nd Group.—The Nailing on of Simple Sticks.

Fig. 5. St. Anthony's Cross.—H. 15, B. 9. The cross-piece is fastened on to the upright with a long nail. The pith of the upright must receive small wooden wedges. (Explain Latin cross, Greek cross, St. Andrew's cross.)

Fig. 6. Latin Cross.—H. 20, B. 8. A round notch can be made in one stick, so that the other may rest firmly in it. Fasten with two nails.

Fig. 7. Interlaced Hurdle.—L. 20, H. 14. The thin ends of willow twigs, useful for nothing else, are employed for interlacing. Put two feet on.

Fig. 8. Stand for flower-pots.—L. 13, B. 9. The sticks nailed one on the other at right angles. Use two nails at each joint.

Fig. 9. *Plant-ladder* to train plants on. H. 38, B. 24, 19, 14.

Fig. 10. *Hurdle.*—L. 24, H. 13. Four hurdles placed together make an enclosure in which sheep may be penned. (Tell some Christmas story about sheep.)

Fig. 11. *Fence.*—L. 14, B. 15.

Figs. 12*a and* 12*b. Easels.*—H. 19, B. above 11, below 14. In Fig. *b* the support is movable. In order to insert a picture or photograph, knock into the lower cross-piece two nails, say, brass-headed ones.

Fig. 13. *Easel* with three vertical pieces. H. 20, B. 13, 16. If we have very thick sticks, we may cut the tops obliquely (as in sketch). The picture may be pasted on to a round piece of cardboard, or board (cut with the fretsaw).

Fig. 14. *Saw-horse.*—Four sticks of equal length (L. 11) are nailed together, two by two, with a long nail; the rail end, coming through, goes into the cross-piece (L. 8). Base as shown.

Fig. 15. *Fruit-basket.* — The bottom is a square board of 7 cm. side (cut with fretsaw). Upon this, along two opposite sides, are nailed sticks (L. 11): on these sticks others (L. 12), and so on. The handle is formed by means of a twig bent as in the sketch.

Fig. 16. *Frame* with double sticks. H. 14, B. 12. Ornamental at top. In order to insert a picture, three sticks pared away obliquely are nailed on behind.

Fig. 17, *a-c. Letters* (HAFEN = harbour). These letters may be nailed on a light-coloured board. H. 8.

3rd Group.—Nailing Simple Sticks *between* Others.

Fig. 18. *Ladder* for tree-frog[1] glass. — L. 18, B. of rungs 4. Wedges in pith part. First nail in position

---

[1] The European tree-frog (Hyla arborea), used in some parts of Europe as a weather guide.

the end rungs and the middle one; then distribute the others.

Fig. 19. *Bier.*—L. 17, B. 4½, H. of legs 2.

Fig. 20. *Post-card holder.*—H. 21, B. 9, 11, H. of front part 9, B. 10.

Fig. 21. *Letter rack* (to be hung up).—H. 20, B. 12.

Fig. 22*a and* 22*b*. *Letter-racks* (to stand on table).— *a*. L. 15, B. 8, H. 12 (compare Fig. 14).—*b*. L. 15, B. 11, H. 9. In the case of *b*, cut the supports off obliquely at the bottom that they may rest firmly on the base.

4th Group.—Half-lapping of Sticks and Staying.

Fig. 23. *Winder.*—L. and B. 14. Both sticks are cut in the middle in the direction of the thickness until the pith is reached. Compare Fig. 74, Plate IX. The sticks, firmly nailed, must lie flat; otherwise, adjust by cutting deeper. The object is used for winding string.

Fig. 24. *Knife-rest.*—L. of the cross-piece 8, H. of crosses 4. A long nail passes through each cross into the cross-piece.

Fig. 25. *Finger-post.*—B. of lower cross 12, H. of upright 16, of the stays 7½; the last are cut away obliquely at the ends. (Bevelling.) The finger part is of paper, cardboard, or wood. Write name to show use.

Fig. 26. *Climbing-frame.*—B. 20, H. 16. The climbing-poles are represented by wooden skewers such as are employed in cork and pea work. (See Appendix.)

Fig. 27. *Swing.*—L. 10, B. 10, H. 16.

Fig. 28. *Railings with Sign-post.*—L. 22, H. of railing 6½, of sign-post 13. The sketch shows two ways in which railings may be joined to make a fence.

Fig. 29. *Table.*—Top has carved outline (3 arcs of circle). Draw an equilateral triangle of 8 cm. side. On each side describe a semicircle. H. of upright 8.

Fig. 30. *Triangle* (for winding string, etc.).—Three equal sticks. L. 14. Oblique half-lapping.

Fig. 31. *Music-stand.*—B. of cross 7, H. 8. Upper square half-lapped at corners (lap-jointed). L. 5, B. 4. Drive a long nail from below through the join of the cross into the upright.

Fig. 32. *Dish-stand.*—L. of cross-piece 10, L. of legs 9. Upper quadrilateral, L. 10, B. $4\frac{1}{2}$. Drive long nails through the lap-joints into the legs. Serves as a stand for dishes; or in the stable, to hold harness.

Fig. 33. *Mirror.*—B. 16, H. 21. A piece of "wood-pulp" is laid behind the mirror-glass. (Press the nails carefully in; do not hammer.) The handle is split into half behind the glass, and nailed on at top and bottom. L. 25.

Fig. 34. *Garden-fence.*—L. 24, B. 15, H. of fence $7\frac{1}{2}$, of gate 7. Gate hinges of leather.

Fig. 35. *Double frame.*—L. 18, H. 12.

5th Group.—Splitting Sticks.

Figs. 36*a* *and* 36*b*. *Geometrical Patterns.*—In splitting the sticks, care is to be taken that the twig is divided into two parts as nearly as possible equal. As soon as we see that one part is thicker than the other, we press with the back of the knife against the thinner half. The rule then is: Always press the back of the blade outwards away from the half which begins to grow the thicker. Practise splitting. In order that the split pieces which are left after practice may not be wasted, they are nailed on to boards in various patterns. The boards so decorated will serve as stands for flower-pots. In 36*a* there are 9 squares. L. of outside edge 9. L. in *b* 10.

Fig. 37. *Garden-fence.*—First cut the two upright sticks, L. 20; then cut the two horizontal ones and split them; L. 15, L. of rails 14.

Fig. 38. *Bridge railing.*—H. 16, B. 15. The sticks which cross each other obliquely, are split. L. of latter 16. For the use of this object see Fig. 49, Plate III.

Figs. 39a and 39b. *Table*, rectangular.—*a*. L. 15, B. 11, H. 8. The top is formed of split twigs. (In the sketch only half is covered.) In *b* the top is a board. L. 20, B. 12, H. 9.

Fig. 40. *Chair*.—H. of seat 6, H. of back 13, B. 6.

Fig. 41. *Garden-seat*.—L. 18, B. $5\frac{1}{2}$, H. of back 13. Make the seat first.

Fig. 42. *Watch-stand*.—H. 15, B. 8.

Fig. 43. *Frame*.— Take good stout sticks and split them. Cross-pieces, L. 19. Uprights, L. 20 and 18.

Fig. 44. *Wheelbarrow*.—L. of the beams 14, B. 4, H. of sloping part $3\frac{1}{2}$. The wheel is sawed out of a piece of board, and has a square axle.

Fig. 45. *Steps*.—L. 12, B. 6, H. $2\frac{1}{2}$, 5, $7\frac{1}{2}$, 10.

Fig. 46. *Fodder-trough*.—L. of side-pieces, which cross each other obliquely, 14, B. 8. To feed the deer.

Fig. 47. *Flower-table*, quadrilateral.—H. 32, edge of top 14. The top is first nailed together, then the hole is chiselled in the middle. By the hole nail two pieces across to secure the sticks which have been cut through by the chisel.

Fig. 48. *Sand-sieve or trap-door*.—L. 19, B. 13, H. 27. The sand sieve is placed slopingly, and the mixed gravel and sand thrown on it. The smaller grains fall through. A trap-door of the form shown is often found in the country districts of Germany. How it falls will be seen from the sketch.

Fig. 49. *Bridge*.—L. 18, B. 6, H. of the posts 12. First make the foot-way, then nail the posts on.

Fig. 50. *Watch-stand*.—L. 14, B. 12, H. 16. A round piece of plush may be glued on under the hook.

Fig. 51. *Portfolio for journals, etc.*—L. of back 20, B. 16, L. of flap 20, B. 15.

Fig. 52. *Flower-stand*, round. Top sawed from a board. Diameter 15, H. 32. Treble staying.

Fig. 53. *Garden-table*.—L. of crossed legs 11, L. of top 12, B. 9.

Fig. 54. Garden-chair.—L. of back and leg together 11, of leg alone 8, B. of chair 5½.

Fig. 55. Wall ornament with match-box in middle.—Set out pattern on a thin board. B. 15, H. 23. Nail the split sticks on. Saw the outline out. Fix the support for the match-box. In the open spaces of the pattern glue dry lichens, moss, birch bark, fir cone scales, acorns, etc. (See Part II.)

6th Group.—Nailing Crosswise.

Fig. 56. Quadrangular prism.—L. 5, B. 5, H. 10. Two rails cross each other at right angles at the points of nailing. A very simple means of joining. Take nails 2½–3 cm. long. Insert wedges in pith part of the cross-pieces. Knock the nails carefully in, 1 cm. from the end of each stick, so that the sticks may not split.

Fig. 57. Blunted square pyramid.—H. 10, L. above 5, below 6, B. as L.

Figs. 58a and 58b. Flower-baskets.—H. 8, B. above 8½, below 5½. Fig. *a* shows three different ways of fastening the side-pieces. In *b*, first make two opposite sides; then nail across pieces of the same length as those that they cross; lastly, nail in the bottom. The baskets may be filled with moss, in which artificial flowers are arranged.

Fig. 59. Fruit-basket, quadrilateral.—L. 14, B. 10, H. 10. First nail the framework together, then nail the side-pieces in.

Fig. 60. Book-stand.—H. 20, L. above 7½, below 13½, B. above 5, below 8.

Fig. 61. " Bird's nest."—L. 10, B. 10, H. 15.

Fig. 62. Doll's cradle.—L. 15, B. 9, H. 10.

Fig. 63. Doll's cradle, with trellis work. Bottom interlaced with thin twigs. (Compare Fig. 7, Plate I.) —L. 20, B. 11, H. 14.

Fig. 64. *Writing-stand.*—L. 16, B. 8, H. of back 9. In the side-openings place two ink-bottles. The tray in the middle is for pens.

Fig. 65. *Market basket.*—L. 11, B. 7, H. 9.

Fig. 66. *Bedstead.*—L. 18, B. 9, H. 10.

Fig. 67. *Bedstead*, bottom interlaced.—L. 20, B. 11, H. 14. (Compare Fig. 63, Plate IV., and Fig. 7, Plate I.)

Fig. 68. *Lounge.*—L. 16, B. 8, H. 8.

Fig. 69. *Canopy-bed.*—L. 16, B. 8, H. 14. A rude bed of this form is found in German villages.

Fig. 70. *Brush-basket.*—L. 7, B. 8, H. 21.

Fig. 71. *Case for one bottle.*—L. 10, B. 10, H. 21. Cut the bottom from "wood-pulp" or a piece of board.

Fig. 72. *Case for four bottles.*—L. 10, B. 10, H. 23. Fix the cross (half-lapped) in position last.

Fig. 73. *Cruet-stand*, for salt and pepper.—L. 10, B. 15, H. 21. Make the frame first; then nail the side pieces in. Bottom of "wood-pulp" or board.

Fig. 74. *Flower-basket stand.* — L. of bottom cross 12, H. of stand 10, L. of basket, below $6\frac{1}{2}$, above $8\frac{1}{2}$, H. 10. Bottom of wood.

Fig. 75. *Triangular prism.*—H. 10, B. 4.

Fig. 76. *Triangular prism with two round slabs.*—H. 10, B. 4. The slabs are sawed from a wood board. Diameter $4\frac{1}{2}$. Will serve as a table.

Fig. 77. *Triangular bottle stand*, prismatic, pyramid-shaped at top.—L. of vertical sticks 15, distance apart 6.

Fig. 78. *Triangular pyramid.*—H. 14, B. 5.

Fig. 79. *Blunted triangular pyramid.*—H. 12, B. below 7, above 4.

Fig. 80. *Blunted triangular pyramid with three round slabs.*—H. 17, B. below 6, above 3. First make the frame; then nail the slabs in. Serves as an étagère.

Fig. 81. *Three-legged stand* (for arrangements of flowers). —Nail the three feet together at the top with one long nail. Spread two out at the front; press one backwards.

Fasten them in position by means of stays. Apply the triangular pyramid at the front (point downwards).

Fig. 82. *Egg-basket*, hexagonal.—H. 12, B. below 7, above 8.

Fig. 83. *Hanging-basket.* (See Fig. 82).—Put a flower-pot with some creeping plant inside and hang up by three cords. The sticks forming the basket are nailed at the bottom to a hexagonal board.

Fig. 84. *Tent*, hexagonal. — H. of uprights 15, B. 8, L. of roof-supports 11. The hinges of the door are strips of leather.

Fig. 85. *Arbour.*—L. 16, B. 12, H. 14.

Fig. 86. *Duster-basket.*—H. of front 12, of back 22, L. of front at bottom 10, at top 11, of back at bottom 12, at top 14, B. above 8, below 6.

Fig. 87. *Fruit-basket*, somewhat long, six-sided.—H. of four uprights in the middle 7, H. of two outer-end sticks 9, B. in middle, at top $6\frac{1}{2}$, at bottom 6, at the side parts B. at top $10\frac{1}{2}$, at bottom $6\frac{1}{2}$. First nail the framework together.

Figs. 88*a and* 88*b*. *Round or hexagonal table*, with three legs.—H. 9, diameter of top (of board) 7. In *b* the strips under the top are indicated by dotted lines.

Fig. 89. *Garden shelter with double seat.*—L. 17, B. 13, H. 14, L. of sloping roof-timbers 7.

Fig. 90. *Basket for worsted ball*, with lid.—H. 9, B. at bottom 6, at top 8. Frame as in Fig. 57. Last of all, nail bottom (of "wood-pulp," board or sticks) in. The lid consists of two cross-pieces on which split twigs are nailed.

Fig. 91. *Shoe-basket.*—B. 5, H. in front 13, behind 11. [Fix door on and call toy bathing-machine.]

Fig. 92. *Basket with lids.*—L. at bottom 16, B. at bottom $10\frac{1}{2}$, H. of handle 24, H. of side-sticks 13, B. at top $10\frac{1}{2}$, L. of sloping sides measured sidewards from the handle 11: the covers must fit in; they are fastened on with strips of leather.

Fig. 93. Flower-pot stand, with three round slabs.—L. of uprights 19, 13, 10.

Fig. 94. Block-house. — L. 20, B. 11, H. 18. First make a strong frame-work. Cut the windows last of all. The sketch exhibits the construction of the frame-work.

7th Group.—Cane Bending.

Fig. 95. Hexagonal basket.—H. 11, upper B. 7. To be able to bend the cane, first beat it carefully with the edge of the hammer. Short pieces are best bent with the round-jawed pliers.

Fig. 96. Flower-pot basket.—H. 12, B. at bottom 5, at top 6. Frame-work as in Fig. 57.

Fig. 97. Sponge-basket.—H. 13, B. at front 15.

Fig. 98. Candlestick.—Diameter 7; the round bottom is cut from a board.

Fig. 99. Table, round, with three legs.—H. 7; diameter at top 6.

Fig. 100. Chair.—H. of back 8, H. of seat $3\frac{1}{2}$, B. 3.

Fig. 101. Match-holder, in the form of a sledge.—L. 20, B. 8. Put a match-box between the two cross bars.

Fig. 102. Smoker's companion.—L. of bottom (board) 23, B. 15. The cigar-holder is hexagonal; the upper rim is of cane bent angularly: H. 9. To the left is the ash-tray, with a small tin plate in the middle; B. 8. To the right there is a contrivance on which a match-box is fixed: H. 7.

B. Work with Split-Wood and Thin Boards.

(Plates VII. to X.)

1st Group.—Cutting of Simple Sticks.

Preliminary Exercises: (*a*) Each pupil receives a piece of wood (say, ordinary firewood) of about 10 cm. in length.

He splits from it three laths, about 2 mm. thick, holding the wood with the left hand and pressing the knife in with the right. Moving the knife slowly to and fro, and at the same time pressing it on, causes the wood to split. The pieces thus obtained are cut smooth with the knife; the direction of the knife is away from the body. Lay the knife flat on the wood so that a long shaving is detached. (Practice in splitting and smoothing short sticks.) Thicker and longer pieces of wood are first split with the axe into smaller sticks.

(b) "Pencil pointing" may again be practised at this point. See exercises (b) and (c) in A.

(c) Vertical cutting through (across) a split stick may be done, if the stick is thin, just as in the case of "natural" wood. With a thick stick we must resort to notching: lay the stick firmly on the table; make a vertical cut with the knife; then notch to that cut from either side. You will at last be able to break the stick. The broken surfaces must be cut smooth. (Practice in vertical and oblique cross-cutting of pieces of wood.)

Fig. 1. *Lath.*—L. 10, B. 1. Take one of the laths obtained by preliminary exercise (*a*): split it to a breadth of 1 cm. and a thickness of 2 mm.; cut it smooth on every side, and finish it with sandpaper. The paper is conveniently left lying on the table, and the wood rubbed to and fro upon it. The finished lath may be used in making a fence, or, if a hole be made in it, as a tree-label.

Fig. 2. *Three parts for a mouse-trap.*—L. 5, 5, 13, B. 1. The sketch shows the make and notching of the sticks. To the long one fasten a piece of bacon. The whole is held together by the pressure of a brick. When the mouse begins to nibble, the trap falls. (For reading choose some story of mice.)

Fig. 3. *Rule.*—L. 25 to 30, B. 1 to 1½. Mark every 5 cm. with a straight notch, every 10 with one straight and two oblique notches.

Fig. 4. *Plant-label.*—L. 7, B. 1½ to 2. Cut the stick smooth, round it at top and point it at bottom. The name of the plant is written on it, and the label is stuck in the flower-pot or flower-bed.

Fig. 5. *Post*, with square cross-section.—L. 12, B. 1. It is employed in Fig. 12.

2nd Group.—Nailing on of Simple Sticks.

Fig. 6. "*Soldier-shears.*"—L. of each stick 12, B. 1. Knock in the nails exactly in the middle and 1 cm. from the end. On the nails mount wooden soldiers; then press the free ends of the shears alternately together and apart. If the soldiers are to wheel, the sticks must be nailed together not in the middle, but 1 cm. to the right or the left of it.

Fig. 7. *Frog-ladder* (see *A*, Fig. 18).—H. 16, B. 5. Tell how the tree-frog is kept in a glass, and used as a weather prophet.

Fig. 8. *Pair of steps.*—H. 16, B. 5. Nail very fast with two brads.

Fig. 9. *Plant-ladder* (for training plants).—H. 40, B. 19, 17, 15.

Fig. 10. *Reading-desk.*—B. 32, H. 20. Nail the front piece of wood, on which the book rests, from the back.

Fig. 11. *Stand for flower-pots.*—L. 10, B. 10.

Figs. 12*a and* 12*b. Fence.*—(*a*) B. 21, H. 19. (*b*) L. of posts 19, of the railings 12, of the cross-bars 17. (The latter may be let in to the posts.)

Fig. 13. *Hurdle.*—L. 16, H. 10. (Compare *A*, Fig. 10.)

Fig. 14. *Folding chair.*—L. of one part 12, of the other 15, B. of chair 5. The seat is made with a strip of cloth.

Fig. 15. *Swing.*—H. 15, B. 10.

Fig. 16. *Horse* (a vaulting-block in a gymnasium).— H. 6, B. 6. (Called, also, a trestle, when used as a support.)

Fig. 17. *Easel.* — H. 15, B. at top 7, at bottom 9. Make the support movable. L. of support 11½.

Fig. 18. *Saw-horse.*—L. of the pieces which cross each other 8, of those which join them 8.

Fig. 19. *Paper-basket.*—H. 12, B. at bottom 6, at top 5. Bottom of board cut with a fretsaw.

3rd Group.—Round Sticks.

Fig. 20. *Stick to wind string on* (*e.g.* for kite-flying).—L. 16. First cut round with the knife, and then smooth with sandpaper.

Fig. 21. *Parcel carrier.*—L. 16. Can also be used to twist a cord tight, etc.

Fig. 22. *Block* to use in tightening the hoops of a cask.—L. 25.

Fig. 23. *Plant stick.*—H. 30.

Fig. 24. *Banner.*—H. 25, L. of cross-piece 9. The paper is glued round the cross-piece. Sometimes used for reserving places at a table.

4th Group.—Thinning away Sticks towards One or Both Sides.

Fig. 25. *Wedge.*—L. 10, B. 2. Of frequent service in fastening the handles of garden tools, hammers, axes, etc. Large wedges are driven into blocks of timber in order to split them.—Round the upper edges of the wedge away. It will then be more durable. Why?

Fig. 26. *Wooden nail* (square cross section).—L. 10, B. 1. Of frequent use in joining beams. The joiner bores round holds in the beams, and drives into them square wooden nails. (Why square?)

Fig. 27. *Round stick or plug.*—L. 12.

Fig. 28. *Paint-brush handle.*—L. 14. Thinned away towards both ends.

Fig. 29. *Dagger.*—L. 22. May be used for opening letters.

Fig. 30. *Sword.*—L. 45, B. 3. For playing soldiers with.

5th Group.—Application of Simple Boards cut with the Fretsaw.

Fig. 31. *Kitchen-shelf.*—B. 10, H. 9, B. of the shelf proper 3. The cross-pieces may be simply nailed on, without cuts being made into which the uprights fit.

Fig. 32. *Table,* four-cornered, four-legged.—L. of top 10, B. 6, H. of legs 6.

Fig. 33. *Chair.*—H. of back 7, H. of front legs 3. The seat is a square of 3 cm. side.

Fig. 34. *Garden-seat.*—L. 12, B. 3, H. of the legs 3, of the back 7.

Fig. 35. *Humming-wheel.*—A circle of wood, 7 cm. in diameter, has two holes bored in it. Through these a string is drawn. Take one end of the string in the right hand, the other in the left. Spin the wheel round so that the string winds itself up. Then draw out and let the wheel hum.

Fig. 36. *Table,* round, three-legged.—Diameter of the top 7, H. of legs 6.

Fig. 37. *Stool.*—Diameter of seat 3, H. of legs 3.

Fig. 38. *Footstool.*—L. of top $3\frac{1}{2}$, B. of same 2, H. of legs or supports 2. The pieces cut out of these are semi-circular in shape. Furniture for doll's house.

Fig. 39. *Flower-stand,* rising by steps.—L. 13, B. 13, H. 9, 6, 4. On the three steps flower-pots are arranged.

Fig. 40. *The same,* to fit into a corner.—B. of side parts $6\frac{1}{2}$, H. 6. The steps are quarters of circles (quadrants). Cut the two side parts from *the same* rectangular board ($8\frac{1}{2}$ long by 6 broad). From the length mark off $\frac{1}{2}$ cm. Then divide the remaining rectangle (8×6) into 12 squares of 2 cm. side. Cut along the sides of squares into two parts. Make the three steps from a board, a quadrant of 6 cm. radius, describing three circles from the same centre at a distance apart of 2 cm.

Fig. 41. *Stand for cask.*—L. 4, H. $3\frac{1}{2}$.

Fig. 42. *Knife-rest.*—Side-parts formed from two squares of 2½ cm. side. In all the sides of the squares a rectangular incision is made. L. of cross-piece 6.

Fig. 43. *Chair with lifting seat.*—L. 5, B. 6½, H. of back 7. The seat is so nailed at both sides that it may be turned up. B. of seat 3½.

Fig. 44. *Garden table.*—L. of top 9, B. 6, H. of legs 7. The latter are nailed to two cross-strips, 6 cm. long, and then fastened under the table.

Figs. 45*a* and 45*b*. *Water-mill.*—(*a*) H. of uprights 12, L. of axle 9, L. of floats 10. (*b*) H. of water stand 12, H. of uprights of wheel 7, L. of axle 6, L. of floats 4. (Divide the surface of the circle into six parts.) On the stand to the left place a tin with a hole in it. Into this hole thrust a stick from which the water may drop.

Fig. 46. *Square.*—L. 5. *Rectangle.*—L. 5, B. 3. *Rhombus.*—L. 5.

Fig. 47. *Circle.*—Diameter 5. *Regular hexagon* and *regular octagon.* Divide the circle into eight equal parts. To do this, draw two diameters at right angles; join their extremities; bisect the joining lines, and draw diameters through the points of bisection.

Figs. 48*a* and 48*b*.—(*a*) *Right-angled triangle.*—L. 10, H. 5. (*b*) *Level*, such as the carpenter (or the potter) uses. Explain the mode of using.

Fig. 49. *Yarn-winder.*—The construction is plain from the sketch. Such an instrument serves for winding yarn, silk, etc. Many different forms of it may be made.

Fig. 50. *Star-wheel.*—Diameter of inner circle 6, of the small outer circles 2½. May be used as a target.

Fig. 51. *Circular ring.*—Diameter 10, B. 2.

Fig. 52. *Crescent.*—H. 20, B. 6. Is set out with the compasses. The radius for the two arcs is the same, the centre different. A small shelf is fixed in the middle, on which some toy figure is placed.

Fig. 53. *Timber-cart.*—L. of beams 16, L. of axle 8, diameter of hind wheel 5, of front wheel 4. The front axle is made to turn on a nail passing through its middle point. The beams may be simply nailed on to the axles instead of let into them.

Fig. 54. *Stool for wash-tub.*—L. 12, B. 6, H. 5.

Fig. 55. *Dining-table*, to pull out.—L. of under-frame 11, B. 7, H. of legs $6\frac{1}{2}$. Make the three parts of the table-top from one piece (L. 18, B. 9). The length of the inserted piece is $6\frac{1}{2}$.

Fig. 56. *Staircase.*—L. of staircase 8, B. 9, H. 8, H. of balustrade 13. The two pieces on which the steps rest are to be cut from one board. The cuts must be at right angles to each other.

Fig. 57. *Cart*, with front and back seats.—L. 8, B. 4, H. $6\frac{1}{2}$. Diameter of wheels 6.

6th Group.—Box-Making (Use of Fretsaw).

Fig. 58. *Open box.*—L. 13, B. 5, H. 4. First nail the four side-pieces together. Join the bottom on last.

Fig. 59. *Money-box.*—L. 8, B. 5, H. 4.

Fig. 60. *Box with espalier.*—L. of box 15, B. 5, H. $4\frac{1}{2}$. H. of espalier 30. Fill the box with earth, and plant in it peas or beans.

Fig. 61. *Box-cart.*—L. of box 12, B. 17, H. 6. Diameter of wheels 8.

Fig. 62. *Crib.*—L. 10, B. 4, 3, H. 9. L. of legs 8.

Fig. 63. *Box with sliding lid.*—L. 12, B. 6, H. 5. Before nailing together, cut the grooves in the two sides. The lid must be pared down on its two longer sides.

Fig. 64. *Dog-kennel.*—L. 8, B. 4, H. 4.

Fig. 65. *Sentry-box.*—L. 5, B. 5, H. 12.

Fig. 66. *Sentry-box inkstand.*—L. 9, B. 6, H. 17, B. of door 6, H. 12. The door is fastened at the bottom to the floor with two hinges. On the inside of the door is nailed a box with a patent ink-bottle ("Normal-Tintenfass") in it.

Fig. 67. *Pump-shaped money-box.*—L. 6, B. 5, H. 11. In front paste a label with the inscription, "No pumping done here." [In German, to "pump" means to borrow money or lend it.]

Fig. 68. *Starling box.* — L. 10, B. 10, H. 18, 14. (Hatching-box for a bird.)

Fig. 69. *Cigar-box converted into a house.*—L. 16, B. 8, H. 14. The flap (of the roof) is fastened with two hinges. The windows and door-frame are made of stained wood.

Fig. 70. *Cupboard.*—L. 14, H. 18, L. of door $8\frac{1}{2}$, H. of same 10. The door is sawed out of the front piece, and fastened at the side with two hinges. For a lock use a bent wire. Behind the front piece nail a box, a little longer and broader than the door-opening.

Fig. 71. *Pen-box.*—L. 21, B. 7, H. 4. The edges and the boards nailed on to the top are decorated by means of chip-carving. First make the outside case, and then fit the drawer-like box into it.

7th Group.—Half-lapping.

Fig. 72. *Angles (right, acute, obtuse).*—L. of the arms 10, B. 1. The breadth of each piece is set off at the end of the other. Cut vertically down the line so obtained; then pare away the wood to half the thickness. (Try square; set bevel.)

Fig. 73a. *Target.* — Diameter 12.   73b. *Target with movable cross.* (When the bull's eye is hit, the cross vanishes.)—Diameter 15, H. of cross 13. The bull's eye is cut and nailed at the bottom of the cross. The cross is fastened with a piece of elastic to the bottom of the target. (Examine the sketches carefully.)

Fig. 74. *Pot-stand.*—L. and B. 13.

Fig. 75. *Grave-cross.*—H. 13, B. 8.

Fig. 76. *Frame.*—L. 12, B. 8.

Fig. 77. *Parallel bars.*—L. of bars 12, H. $6\frac{1}{2}$. In the supports, L. of pieces running lengthways 14, of cross-pieces $8\frac{1}{2}$.

Fig. 78. *Windmill.*—L. of each pair of arms 20.

Fig. 79. *See-saw.*—L. of cross-beam 30, H. of frame 5.
Fig. 80. *Merry-go-round.*—L. and B. 30.
Fig. 81. *Dove-cot*—H. of upright 12, cross-pieces 11: L. of cot 4, B. 4, H. 6.
Fig. 82. *Mangle.*—L. 22, B. 8, H. of middle post 13: L. of rolling box (filled with stones) 21, B. 6½, H. 4.

8th Group.—Cutting along Curves; Drawing partly Freehand.

Fig. 83. *Spatula.*—L. 18, B. 4. (A spade-shaped tool used in clay modelling.)
Fig. 84. *Toy banner* "Engaged."—H. 20. (Used to reserve seats at a public table.)
Fig. 85. *Console.*—Top semicircular, diameter 14. H. of support 11, B. 6.
Fig. 86. *Watch-stand.*—B. 7, H. 10. Below the hook glue a round piece of plush.
Fig. 87. *Plush ellipse* and *oval* (true egg-shape).—L. 18. A simple method of construction may be used for the ellipse. Fix two nails for the foci. Pass a string loosely about them, and trace the ellipse with a pencil held so as to keep the string always at full stretch. For the oval draw two circles, a larger and a smaller, some little distance apart. Join them at the sides by free curves which blend with the circumferences of the circles. (More difficult constructions would be out of place with younger boys.)
Figs. 88a *and* 88b. *Leaves.*—L. 16, B. 12. Various forms may be cut. (To be used as fruit-plates.)
Fig. 89. *Litter.*—L. of box 6, B. 4, H. 3½. L. of poles 18. (Something like an old-fashioned litter.) German workmen use such boxes to carry sand and stones.
Fig. 90. *Doll's cradle.*—L. 15, B. 8, H. 14. Fit the bottom in last.
Fig. 91. *Key-board.* B. 12, H. 16.
Fig. 92. *Gymnast* (Leotard).—H. of frame 20, B. 4½.

H. of gymnast 12. If the gymnast, head downwards, is fastened with worsted to two points on either side of the frame, and the frame is pressed together at the bottom, the gymnast will turn over.

Fig. 93. *Stamp-box.*—L. 6, B. 4½, H. 2, 7. The cover is fastened with a nail at each side so as to lift up and down.

Fig. 94. *Sofa.*—L. 8, B. 4, H. 7.

Fig. 95. *Wheelbarrow.*—L. 25, B. 5, H. 5. Diameter of wheel 4½.

Fig. 96. *Toy-cart.*—L. of bottom 12, B. 6, H. of back 8, of front 4, diameter of wheels 6, 5. The front axle is movable.

Fig. 97. *Rattle.*—The middle part is fixed to the handle: the two outer parts only joined to it with a piece of twine. B. of middle part 4, H. 12.

Fig. 98. *Egg-crate.*—L. 16, B. 12, H. 18. First make the prism-shaped framework, then nail on the side sticks and the bottom.

Fig. 99a *and* 99b. *Sledges.*—(a) L. 10, B. 4, H. 4. (b) L. of runners 16, B. 6.

Fig. 100. *Crossbow.*—L. of whole 30, B. 2, H. 2½. Saw first the two side-parts with slits in them (L. of slit 20).

Fig. 101. *Pig.*—L. 20.

Appendix

Course in Paper, Cardboard, and Stick Work.

(First Preparatory Stage. Plate XI.)

Introductory Note.

The course partly represented in Plate XI. has grown by degrees in the Berlin school-workshops during many years. The objects are, for the most part, connected with Frœbel's practical "occupations" for the Kindergarten, and are a further development thereof. They thus offer nothing essentially new. Peculiar to the course are only the arrangement and grouping, which are such that progress is carefully graduated. The value of the order adopted has been proved by the test of practice.

We are the less inclined to give elaborate instructions for making the several objects, as quite a literature has already been devoted to the various groups we now present. Besides the works mentioned in the Introduction, we may call attention to Kalb's *Der erste Unterricht in der Knabenhandarbeit*[1]: Hertel's *Papierarbeiten*, for boys of from eight to fifteen; and Barth and Niederley's *Des Kindes erstes Beschäftigungsbuch*.

We confine ourselves to making general observations after each group, and give in the last plate representations only of a few selected objects from each group.

[1] An edition with supplementary exercises has been published in English by Messrs. Newmann & Co.

Course.

1st Group.—Cutting Pictures off and out.

Practice in the use of the scissors by guiding them along given lines or contours.

The ordinary picture sheets, on which the several pictures are divided from each other by lines, are first pasted on to strong paper. The pupils begin by cutting strips; they then cut the single pictures from the strips. Afterwards the outlines of the beasts, soldiers, etc., are cut out.

It pleases the boys if they may fix the figures by means of a creased strip of paper to a piece of cardboard or " woodpulp," and so make them stand.

2nd Group.—Folding, the Primary Figure being a Square or Rectangle.

Practice in the use of the scissors by guiding them along lines drawn by the children themselves. Practice in measuring; also in folding.

A rectangular sheet of paper, 20 (afterwards 40, 80) cm. wide, and of any length, is divided by folding into 2 (afterwards 4, 8) long strips: on these squares (afterwards rectangles) are measured off, cut off, and then used for folding.

The well-known folding exercises of the Kindergarten have been brought into sequence as follows:—(*a*) Square: envelope, basket without and with decorations, pepper and salt holder, imperial crown, windmill, boats, ships, birdboxes, thread-winder, *jacket*.[1] (*b*) Rectangle: hat, wallpocket, magic pocket-book, boat, arrow, letter-book, flapper. Example: Plate XI., to right, Fig 2.

[1] When the name of an object is printed in italics, there is a representation of it on Plate XI.

3rd Group.—Forming Figures by Mounting Squares and Rectangles.

Practice as before; also, practice in mounting; training of the senses of form and colour. Applied net-drawing. On drawing sheets with net-lines (*i.e.* ruled in squares), first squares, then rectangles are arranged systematically into figures. This is in connexion with drawing on ruled sheets. Most simple drawing copies may here be usefully employed. The same figure may be repeated several times. The making of the squares (side generally 2 cm.) and rectangles which must fit into the net, is, as in group 2, by the pupil himself. The employment of variously-coloured paper is highly to be recommended. The colours are indicated in Plate XI. by different methods of shading. Thick paper or thin cardboard will be found most suitable for the work. For pasting on, use starch or dextrine.

This group offers great variety. Examples may be seen in Plate XI., to left, Figs. 1–6.

4th Group.—Small Objects of "Pressed Straw" or "Wood Pulp."

Made by measuring, folding, and cutting in square. Examples: simple sweet-bag, wind-mill, Christmas-tree chain, perforated chain, tuft, apple-net, nut-bag, *basket*. (Plate XI., to right, Fig. 3.)

5th Group.—Wood with Thin Cardboard, based on the Square and the Rectangle.

Conversion of surfaces into solids.

Made are:—square tables and rectangular boxes, baskets and trays in great variety. As examples, we give on Plate

XI., to right, Figs. 4-6: a simple square basket, a rectangular tray, and a box with lid.

6th Group.—Formation of Figures by Mounting Squares and Rectangles in combination with Triangles.

As in Group 3. Additional are the triangles, which are obtained by dividing squares along the diagonals. Examples: Plate XI., to left, Figs. 7-11.

7th Group.—Simple Plaiting and Weaving.

Practice in the use of the knife by guiding it along an iron ruler (or try square).

The knife here makes its appearance for the first time. The strips cut with the knife—they should not be less than 1 cm. in width—are neater and truer than those cut with the scissors. We may make: various *book-markers* (Plate XI., to right, Fig. 7), weaving nets, crosses, mats, hearts.

8th Group.—Work with Paper and Thin Cardboard, based on the Circle and Regular Polygons.

Practice in the use of the compasses.

Made are:—serpent, circular, *square*, hexagonal, octagonal, etc., hanging baskets, double sweet-bags, candle-guards, *hexagonal*, octagonal, duodecagonal trays (Plate XI., to right, Figs. 8 and 9).

9th Group.—Formation of Figures by Cutting out and Mounting Free Forms. Forms taken from Life.

Examples: Plate X., to right, Figs. 12–15.

Groups 3, 6, and 9 admit of many variations of form, and may be developed to an endless extent. We have found them of very great assistance to the teaching of the class-room in the first preparatory stage.

Those of the pupils who have finished first some piece of work on which all are engaged, take their drawing sheets, which always lie at hand, and produce from copies or invent combinations of forms, until all are ready to begin some new work. Such exercises give great pleasure to the more skilful boys, and have a good effect on their taste and fancy.

10th Group. — Composite Work, on a larger scale, to Revise and Fix what has already been Learnt.

Woven mats, pasted on to "wood-pulp," with borders. Woven baskets, lamp-stands, targets, etc. (Table XI., to right, Figs. 10 and 11.)

11th Group. — Ornaments for hanging on a Christmas Tree, made from Cardboard Patterns.

The patterns are to be had from scholastic publishers, especially at Christmas time. It is advisable to make the patterns stronger by mounting them on fairly thick paper. To "scratch," that is, to remove part of the thickness where the crease is to come, use a knife. (Plate XI., to right, Fig. 12.)

12th Group.—Cork and Stick Work.

This group forms the transition to Easy Wood-Work.

The use of corks to join the sticks together has been found more advantageous than that of peas. Still better are the metal tubes specially designed for this purpose. The cost of 1000 corks is 4s.; other round sticks can be obtained for sixpence. The products of cork work are:—
(a) angles, (b) geometrical figures, (c) geometrical solids, (d) forms derived from life—tables, chairs, letters, houses, etc.

Lastly, the sticks may be employed in combination with "wood-pulp" to make hurdles, seats, baskets, or other receptacles. Examples: Plate XI., to right, Figs. 13–18.

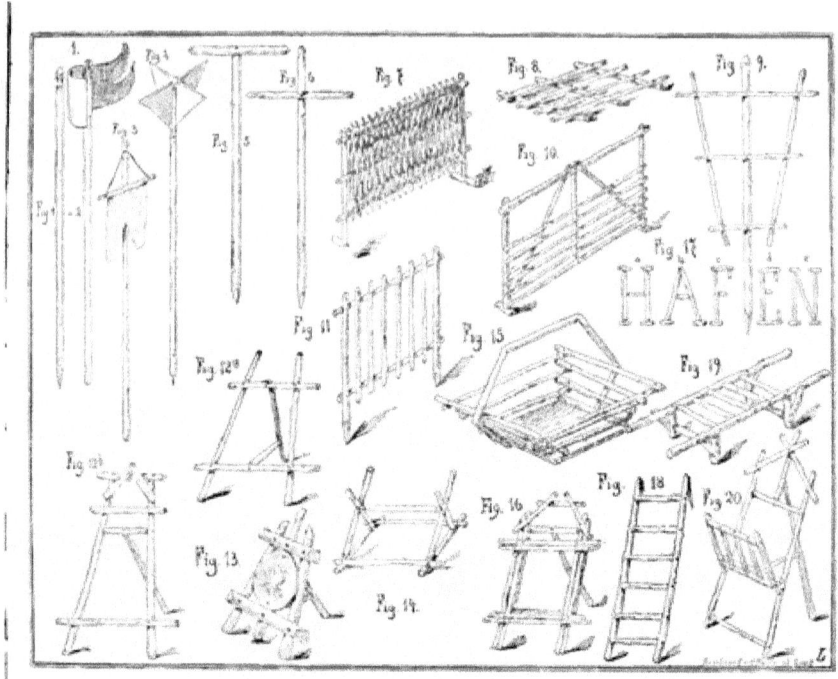

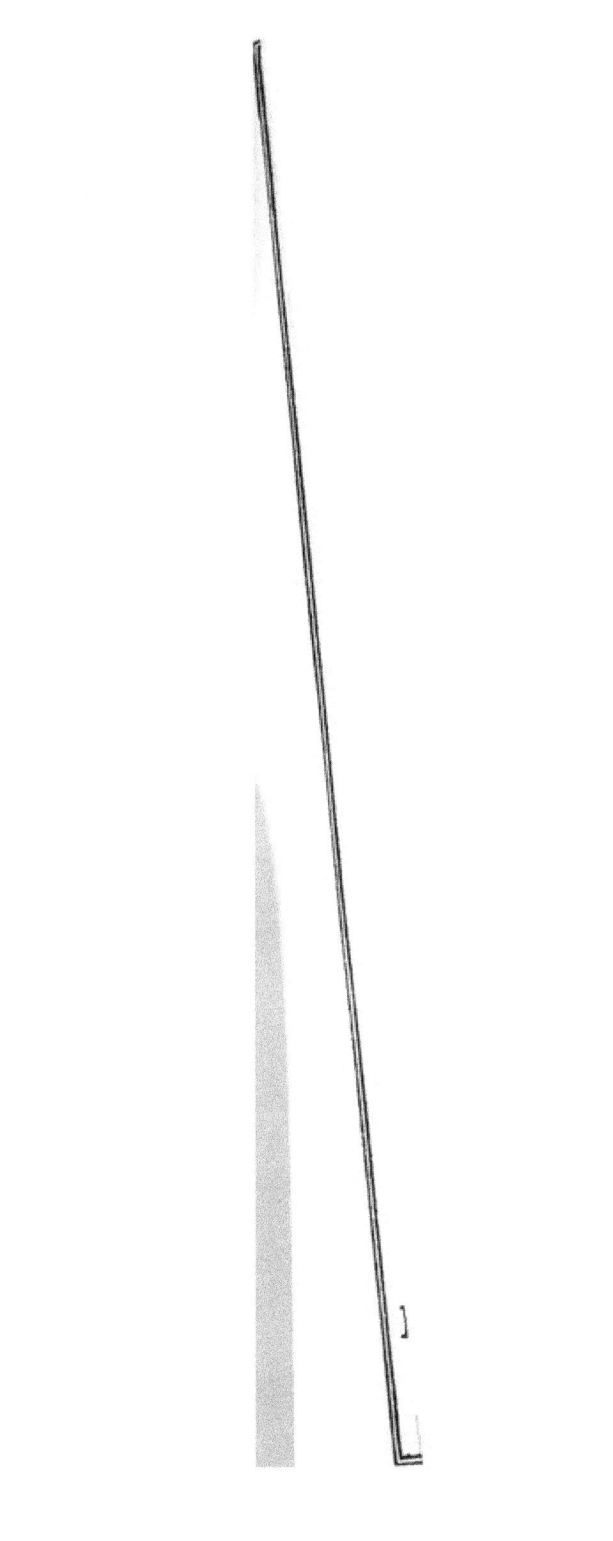

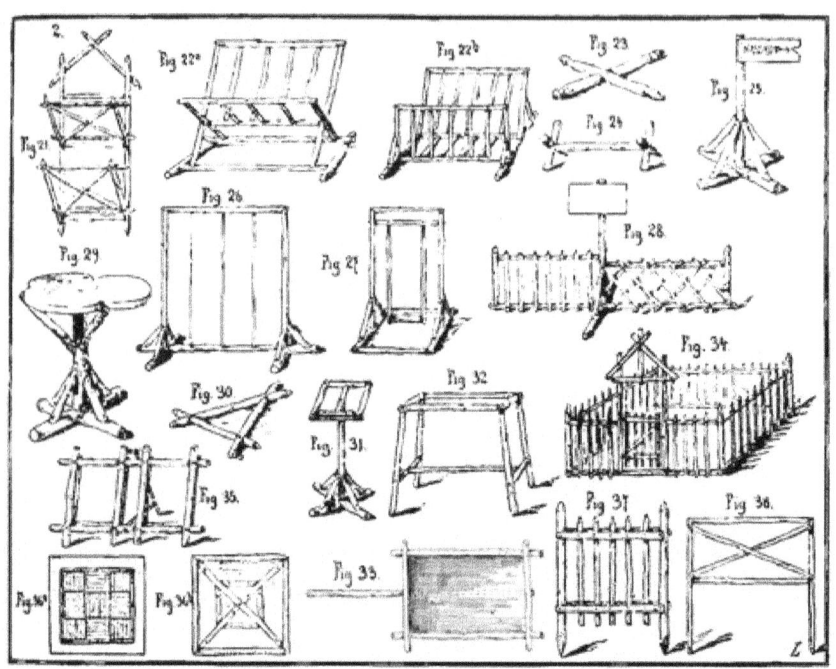

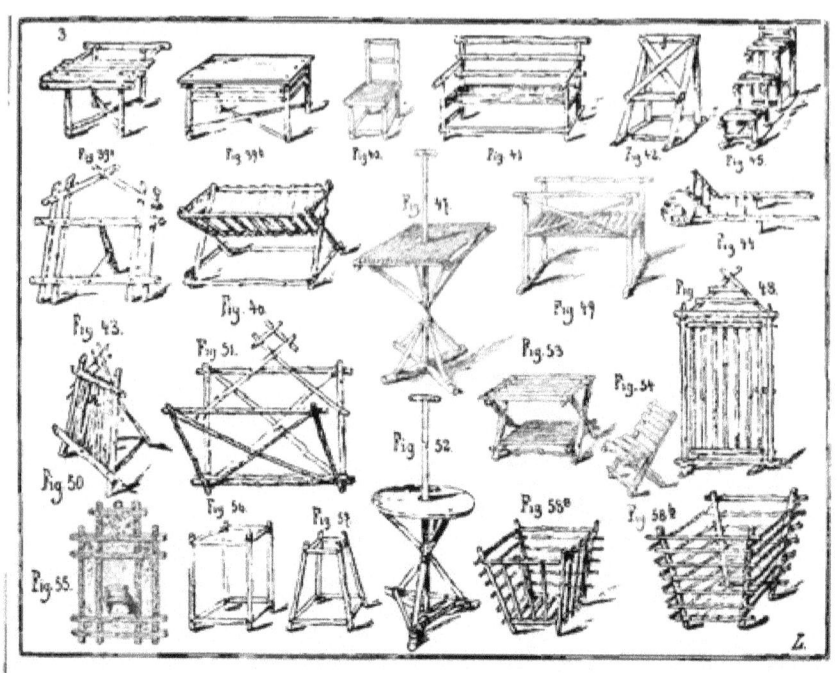

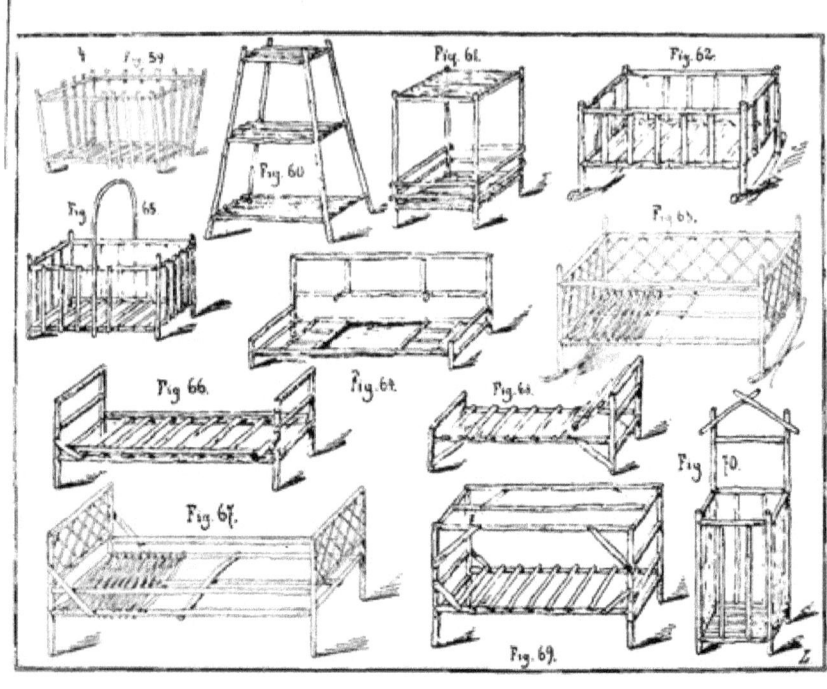

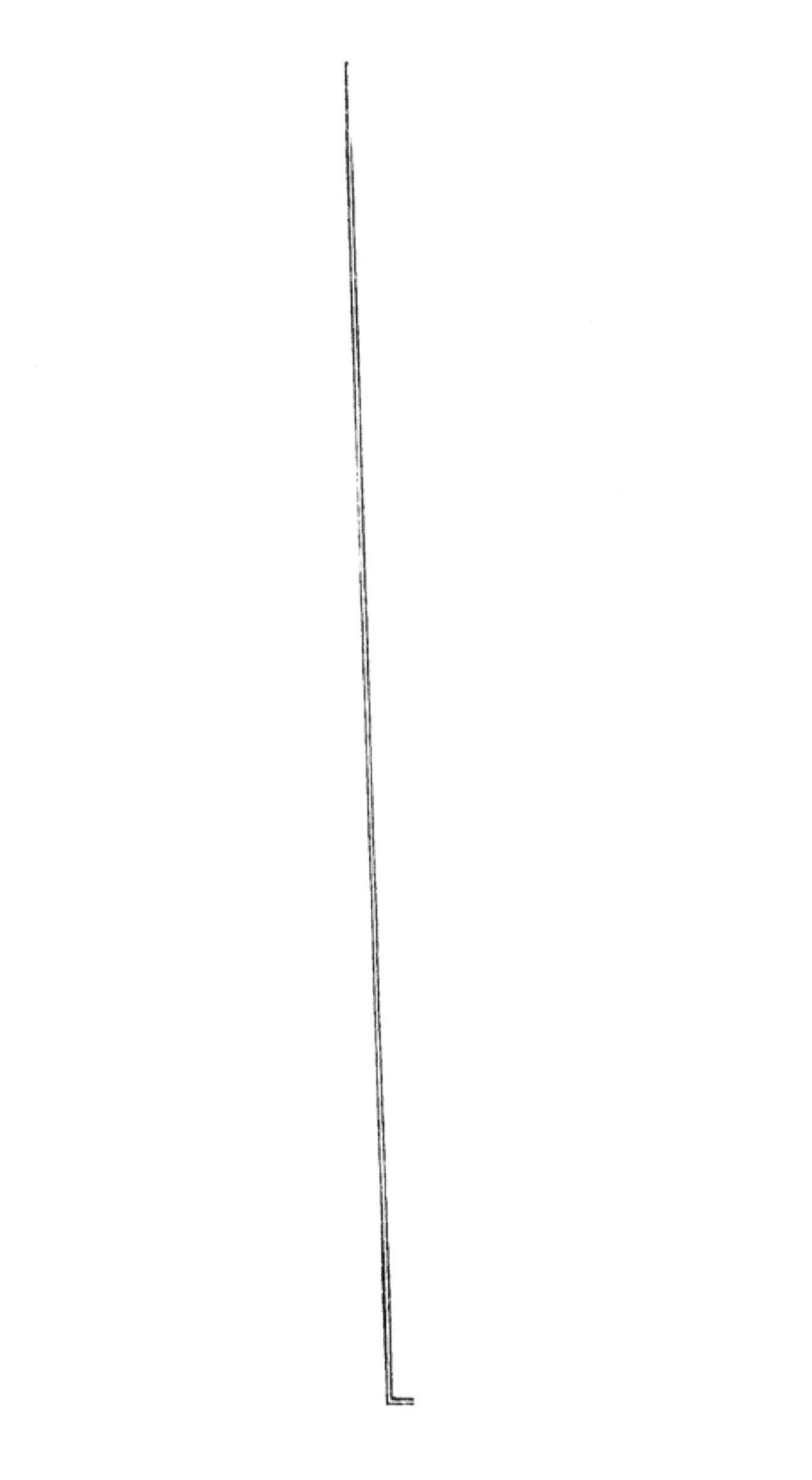

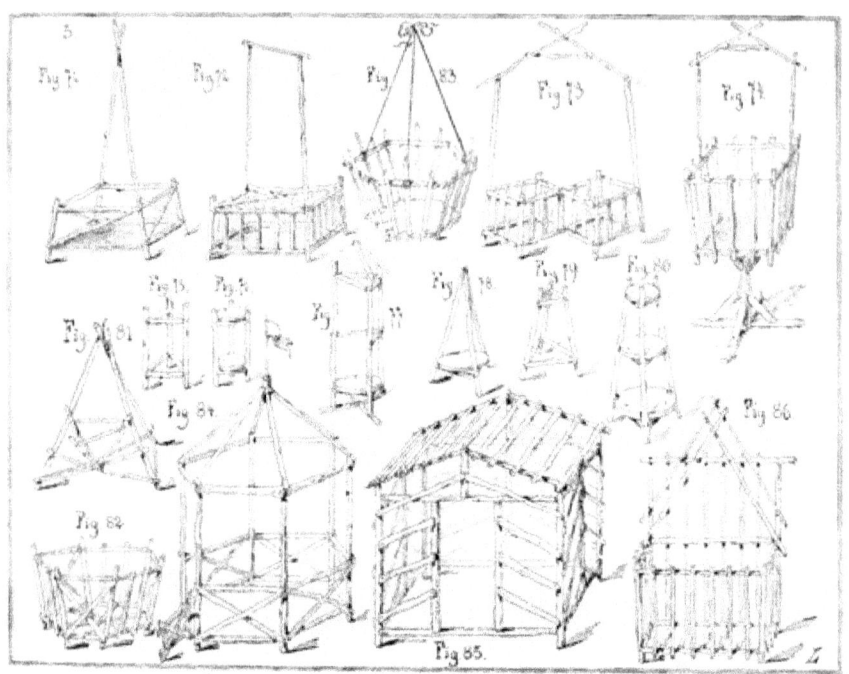

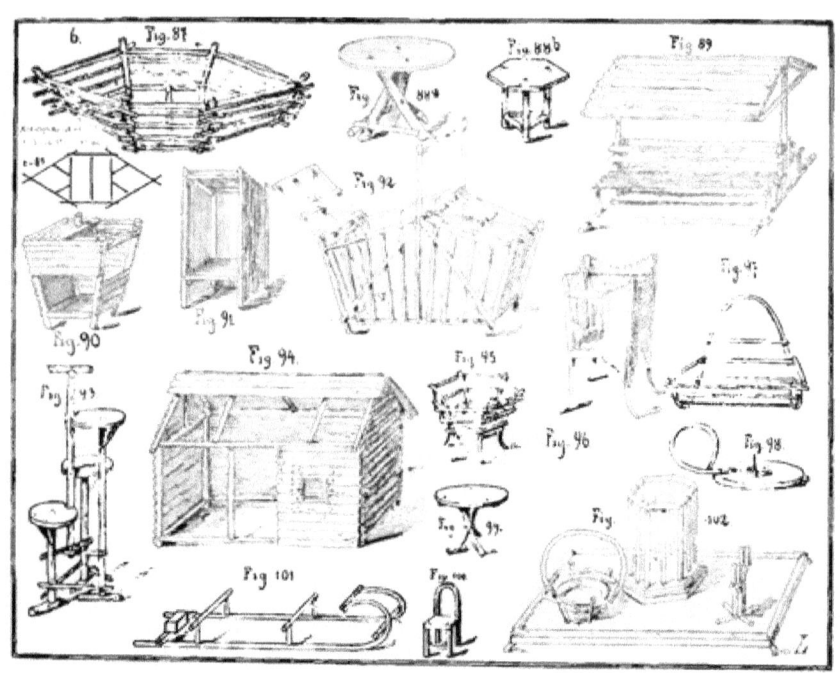

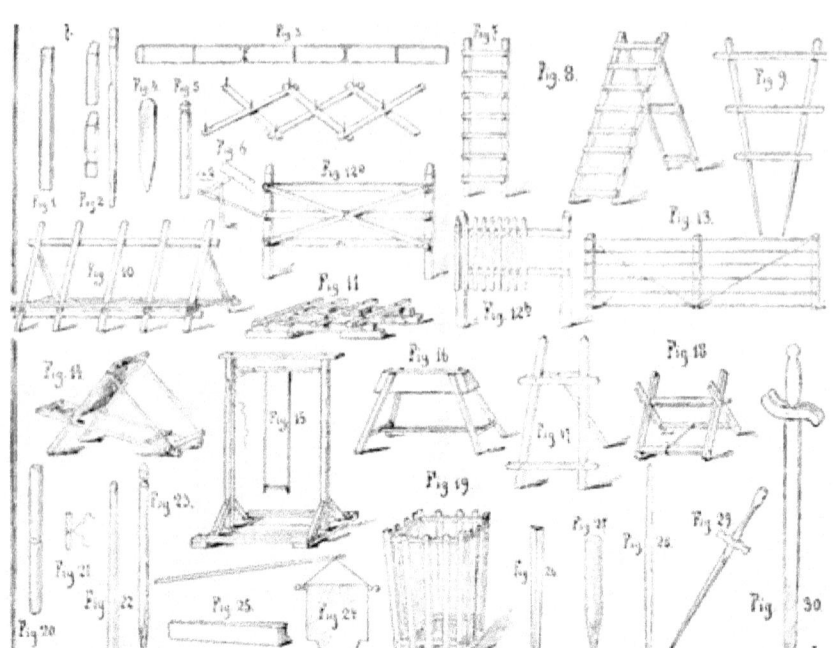

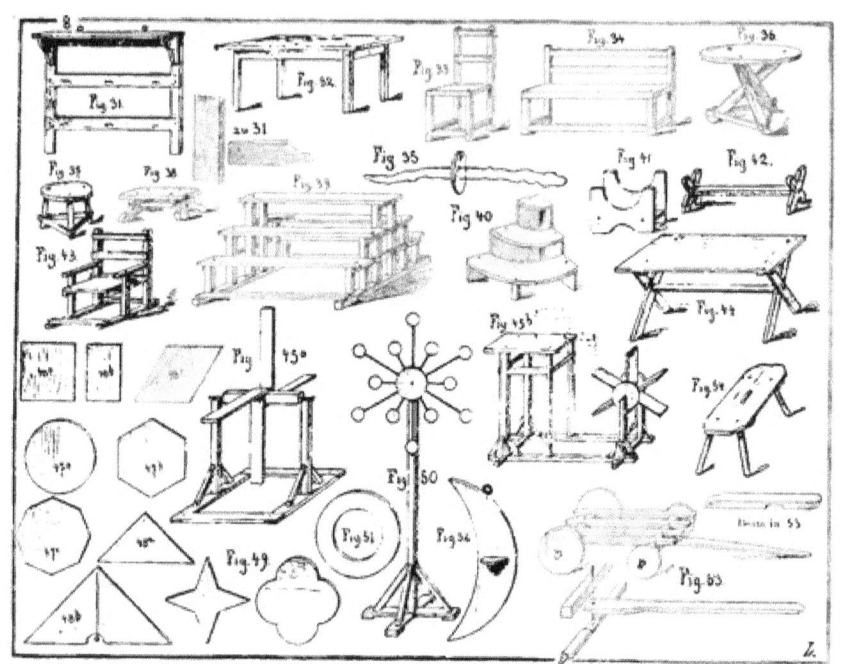

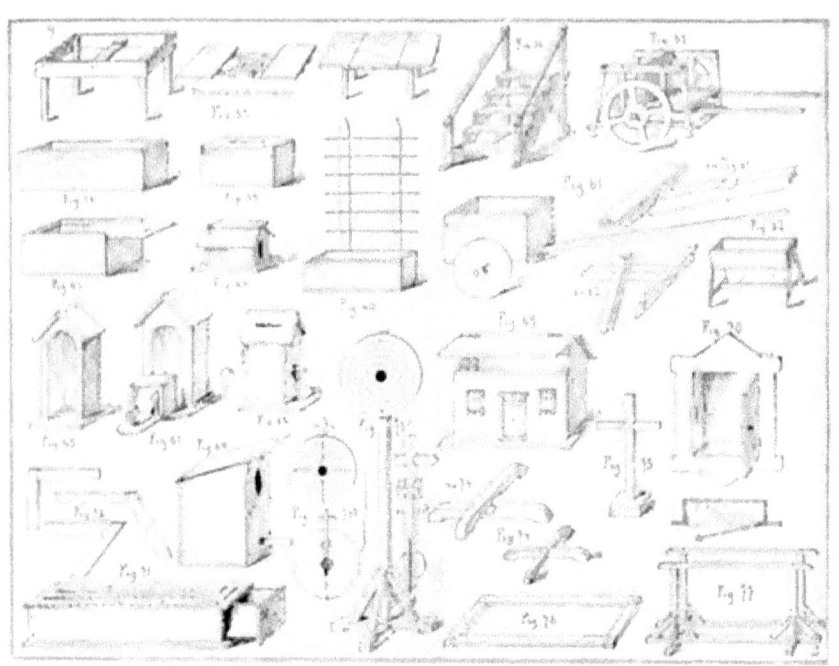

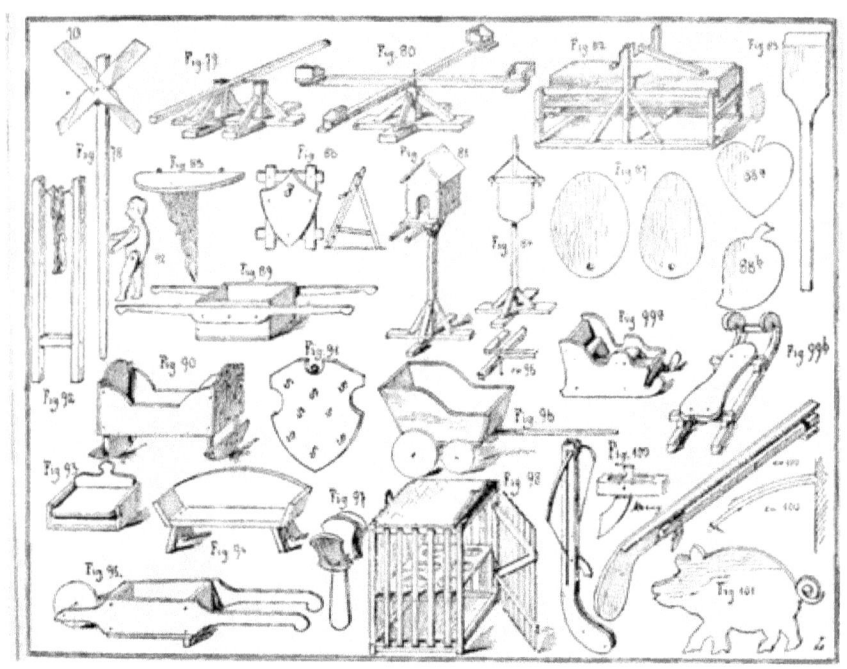

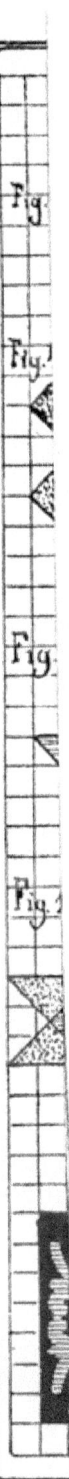

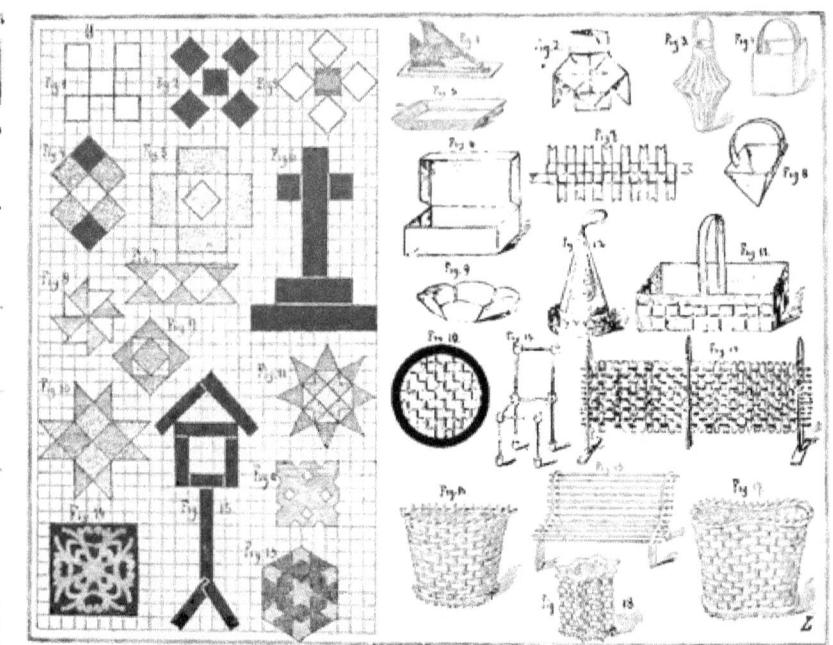

www.ingramcontent.com/pod-product-compliance
Lightning Source LLC
Chambersburg PA
CBHW031609110426
42742CB00037B/1465